Jeffrey Lampkin

INSIDE OUT

A 21 day spiritual consecration that invites you on a wondrous journey for truth and transformation

Inside Out
© 2025 by Jeffrey Lampkin

All rights reserved. No part of this book may be reproduced, stored, or transmitted in any form or by any means—electronic, mechanical, photocopying, recording, or otherwise—without prior written permission from the publisher, except for brief quotations in reviews.

ISBN: 979-8-9928515-0-2

Cover Design: KaDarrius Ellerbe and Kalon Studios
Interior Formatting: Nauman Akbar (@NaumanAkabar269)
Editor: Gwendolyn Baker

Published by MD Publications, MDPubs.World

Printed in the United States of America

Dedication

This book is dedicated to every **SURVIVOR**! If you're reading this, you have literally **SURVIVED** what others have died from. So, for every day that you fought and wrestled with insecurities, poor decisions, and the idea that you wouldn't be able to change, I dedicate this book to **YOU**!

The fact that you picked up this book says that something inside (**Jesus**) keeps reminding you that **CHANGE is ALWAYS possible.**

Welcome Home 🙏🖤

Start Strong
Bishop Simeon Moultrie

One of my favorite scriptures is Joshua 1:7-8: "*Only be strong and very courageous, that you may observe to do according to all the law which Moses My servant commanded you; do not turn from it to the right hand or to the left, that you may prosper wherever you go. This Book of the Law shall not depart from your mouth, but you shall meditate in it day and night, that you may observe to do according to all that is written in it. For then you will make your way prosperous, and then you will have good success.*"

This moment in scripture is powerful. Joshua is stepping into leadership after the death of Moses and the weight of responsibility is heavy. The pressure is real, but his purpose is even greater. This is a new season for him and God is making it clear: START RIGHT!

You've probably heard the saying, "*It's not where you start, but where you finish.*" While that's true in many ways, how you start still matters. Think about a race. In track, a strong start can set you up for victory. It builds momentum and confidence. If there's one thing the enemy wants to shake, it's your confidence.

That's why this consecration isn't just about finishing strong; it's about starting strong, locking in, staying focused, and refusing to get distracted. Don't veer off course and keep your eyes forward. God has promised that you will prosper wherever you go, if you stay the course.

So, as you go through this consecration, speak the Word over your life, meditate on what God is revealing to you and remain vigilant because clarity is key in this season.

I'm praying over you, believing that what God does in your life during this time will be nothing short of amazing!

Let's get started!

Song of the Day:
Jesus Is My Help
Hezekiah Walker & The Love Fellowship Choir

Table of Contents

DAY 1	01
DAY 2	03
DAY 3	05
DAY 4	07
DAY 5	10
DAY 6	13
DAY 7	16
DAY 8	17
DAY 9	20
DAY 10	23
DAY 11	26
DAY 12	29
DAY 13	32
DAY 14	36
DAY 15	38
DAY 16	41
DAY 17	44
DAY 18	49
DAY 19	52
DAY 20	55
DAY 21	58

Day 1

Good Morning LampNation♥Consecration Is here🙏🙏. WOW! This entire project is a GOD led, GOD inspired, GOD directed offering to Him. I yield myself to Him and whatever it is that He wants to do at this moment. This is the mantra that I desire for all of you to have. This is the posture that we must be in as we take this journey. Total freedom in Christ should be our goal. Join me for the next 21 days as we give ourselves back to GOD. It's time to clean out and detox. There are SO MANY distractions In this world and you must build your spirit and remain in control with God! "This Can Be Your Year But You Must Do Your Work". If you are like me, this can be scary. You might say, "Jeffrey, I want to please God and I want to go higher, but I know it's going to separate me from some things that I love. It's going to separate me from some things that my flesh enjoys. That's scary because it's like I'm moving into a new norm." However, I'm reminded, in Matthew 16:26, "For what will it profit a man if he gains the whole world (wealth, fame, success), but forfeits his soul? Or what will a man give in exchange for his soul?" You are making a decision today to choose GOD. To choose the plan that He has for your life.

I can't tell you that this journey will be easy, but with GOD all things are possible.

#RemoveTheDistractions#LaserFocus#WithGodICan
#BeInTheWorldNotOfThe World.

> "Be sober [well balanced and self-disciplined], be alert and cautious at all times. That enemy of yours, the devil, prowls around like a roaring lion [fiercely hungry], seeking someone to devour."
> **1 Peter 5:8 AMP**

**Song of the Day:
Song of Consecration-Bishop Paul S. Morton**

Day 2

As I was studying this morning, my heart rang out "Wash Me Over Again, with your precious blood, wash me over again." Do you realize that we need to wash DAILY! We need to cleanse our bodies because it refreshes us and we feel renewed. It's a process but when it happens, we feel BETTER. Just because we accept the Lord doesn't mean we don't need consecration and renewal which will cleanse us from unrighteousness. We are sinners and we sin daily, BUT God is God and because we abide in Him and He in us, we can CONFESS and admit to Him forcefully, "I messed up." He can cleanse us and change our NATURE. Lord knows I sin...whew!

In 1st John, it says,

"If we [freely] admit that we have sinned and confess our sins, He is faithful and just [true to His own nature and promises], and will forgive our sins and cleanse us continually from all unrighteousness [our wrongdoing, everything not in conformity with His will and purpose]."
1 John 1:9 AMP

Notice that word, CONTINUALLY!! Daily we must confess and trust God to forever cleanse us. We were caterpillars, but He performed a METAMORPHOSIS and now we are beautiful BUTTERFLIES. We need cleansing so we can stay pure and the only one who can cleanse us is JESUS. Thank God for the cleansing. So, take a moment and say, God wash me over again. I used to sing this song all the time, yep, I'll be singing it all day. Have a great day my Loves🙏🖤!

#WashMeOverAgain   #DailyIWorship   #SeekHimDaily #Consecrate

Song of the Day:
Wash Me Over Again-Rev. Timothy Wright & Dorinda Clark-Cole

Day 3

You may ask, "Jeffrey, what's really the point of this consecration? This period of denial? Am I really going to be transformed?" Well, my beloved, what do you believe in your heart? I believe that God can truly cleanse us of our struggles and renew us in this journey called life. We must spend time with Him and allow Him to change us from the inside out. Part of this is going before God Full and Free. He already knows us. Take off the mask and cry out "HELP Me, God, I need you." Give me the strength I need and send the RIGHT support. Ask Him, "Help me know You are real." and He will do it.

This morning I was reading about Moses as he was writing the Ten Commandments. After spending time with God and receiving revelation (which is what happens when you abide in Him - witty ideas that were mind-blowing), When Moses came out there was a glow so bright on his face, he put on a veil. But when he went before God, he removed it.

> "But whenever Moses went in before the Lord to speak with Him, he would take off the veil until he came out. When he came out and he told the Israelites what he had been commanded [by God],"
> **Exodus 34:34 AMP**

As you are in consecration, take off your mask. Give God "The Real Real." He already knows, but He needs you to confess it and believe that only He and He alone can deliver the necessary change. Here's the beauty- when you go in as a caterpillar, you come out as a butterfly - so beautiful and free because God's glory is shining. Through the consecration, as you encounter people, I pray that His countenance shines upon you so heavy that they really say, "Wow, you're glowing. "Yes, because I'm pregnant with every possibility God has for me. I'm getting ready to birth His will, His Plan, and His Desire for me". God, I feel this thing today. My beloved, Get in His Presence and go beyond the veil! Have A Light Shining Day 🙏🖤❗

#HisLightIsMyLight #TheWeightOfGlory #BeyondTheVeil

**Song of the Day:
Beyond the Veil-Daryl Coley**

Day 4

Isn't it amazing how you can literally exist, but not be operating at your maximum potential? How you can have a car and when you wash it, wax it and give it an oil change, it seems to run better? Or maybe you had a suit or dress that after a good wash and press, you put that bad boy on and looked like new money. Hmmmm, they all go through a process, but come out better than they were before. You just need a transformation filled with love and care, but a detox of impurities has to take place in order for this change to come about.

Transformation is a process and it takes time. The car needed the mechanic, the clothes needed the washing machine and a good hot iron, and YOU needed time with God to transform you, to show you yourself and to hear His voice for the plans that He has for YOU. The world can distract us so greatly to make us want to be and appear like them. We hear what they say and move how they move.

We speak their words and all the while God is saying, "But what did I say?" In order to hear God, we must remove ourselves from the everyday distractions of the world and allow God to speak to us and transform us in HIS image. There are two frequencies that are taking place- The world and God. What frequency are your ears connected to? Are you more concerned with following the latest trends and being popular or is your heart and mind yearning to be fully transformed into the image that God has in mind for you. If you need to know God's plan for your life, get in the spirit and let the Lord minister to you. During this time of consecration, yield to the will of God. God not my will but YOUR will be done.

> "But whenever a person turns [in repentance and faith] to the Lord, the veil is taken away. Now the Lord is the Spirit, and where the Spirit of the Lord is, there is liberty [emancipation from bondage, true freedom]. [Is 61:1, 2] And we all, with unveiled face, continually seeing as in a mirror the glory of the Lord, are progressively being transformed into His image from [one degree of] glory to [even more] glory, which comes from the Lord, [who is] the Spirit."
> **2 Corinthians 3:16-18 AMP**

You've been feeling heavy and overwhelmed because you're trying to move and live life your way, but there is a freedom when we move God's way. Changing isn't easy, but God will equip you and empower you when you spend time with Him.

With Him there is freedom and liberty because you know you're doing this thing called "life, His way. Remove the veil and come to God and allow HIS glory to carry you to higher heights. Get in the spirit my beloved, hear on the frequency of God, and let the Lord minister to you.

#ChangeYourDial#GetInTheSpirit#ChangeMeOhGod #InsideOut

Song of the Day:
Let The Lord Minister To Ya
Donald Lawrence & The Tri-City Singers

Day 5

If you are like me, at this point I'm beginning to see and feel a change. Isn't it beautiful to be intentional about being a vessel that God can use? He created us and He knows our inner most thoughts and deeds. I find myself in this period of consecration desiring to hear Him more. The detox from social media or other music has aided me in being able to hear and see things clearly. WOW! How distracted are we really as humans! Limiting can release weight and freedom. But don't get it twisted…all of this wisdom and insight is not Jeffrey, it's God. As you change and feel more sanctified (lol oh you feeling mighty Holy lol) you must realize this is simply so God can be glorified in the Earth. We are simply being equipped to be the hands and feet of Jesus.

Today's daily reading is about John the Baptist and how he stated,

"A man can receive nothing, except it be given him from heaven."
John 3:27 KJV

This moment, this transformation, this change is God's doing so you can go out and be an Ambassador of Christ. Loving the way He loves, giving the way He gives, speaking the way He speaks. It's About HIM. He has the power to make you great as you make His name great and compel a dying world to come back to Him and truly honor Him as Lord of Lords. John the Baptist went on to say,

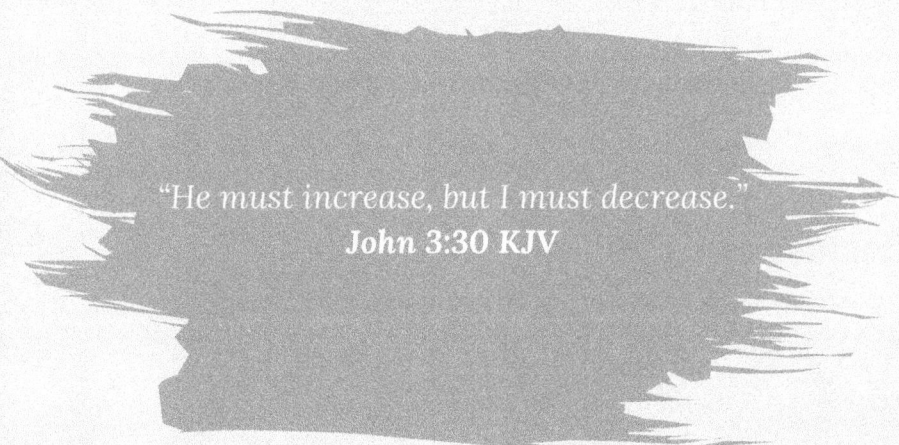

"He must increase, but I must decrease."
John 3:30 KJV

Anybody grateful that God is trusting you to carry out His plans here on the earth?

Isn't it amazing how God used His servant to complete His work? John the Baptist was in the wilderness teaching and preaching the Word. He was refined, purified by God, and in the posture of a servant. In the wilderness, He used a servant who never at any moment made it about himself, but understood that the will of the Lord must be done. There is a work God wants to do through you, BUT God must be the biggest and most important thing in your world. Not your spouse, child, family, job, because all these blessings come from God. God should be at the center of it all. And when you find God at the center, you will find balance and your life will feel more in tune.

These 21 days are about allowing God to center our hearts and our minds and purify us with His cleansing spirit so we can be lights in this dark world. As I always say, "And because God is the Greatest Power, we shall not be defeated." Shine Jesus Shine
#GodIsTheGreatest #PurifyOurHearts
 #TheWeightOfGlory

Song of the Day:
Clean Me Up-O'Landa Draper Associates

Day 6

So you've made the commitment to God to be renewed and to increase your faith and really be in this race for God. As you are reading the Word, fasting, praying (a little more than normal) you're feeling sanctified, right?? And then good old temptation comes a knocking. You've been consistent, but Lord you just so hungry before it's time for your fast to end, or that new non-gospel song just dropped and everyone is talking about it. You want to listen, but you made a commitment to yourself and God. Jeffrey, this is becoming exhausting! Well first, STOP and BREATHE. Okay, are you alright?? Because that breath you just took should be a reminder that God is still with you and because He is, this journey is still possible. Understand this my beloved, your sinful nature is natural and it's real.

David said in Psalm 51:5,

> *"Surely I was sinful at birth, sinful from the time my mother conceived me."*
> **Psalms 51:5 NIV**

We are all born into sin. We are flesh and we are all sinful in nature. Even great writers of the word dealt with sin. Apostle Paul talks about it in Romans 7 and David made reference in Psalms 51. It's sad to say, but our hearts are inclined towards evil. That's why this transformation from God is so critical. We can't do this on our own; however, here is the beauty in all of this. While I am yet a sinner, Christ died on the cross and freed me from the bondage of my sins. You have been delivered and freed by the blood of the Lamb.

John put it so eloquently in the book of Revelation when he said

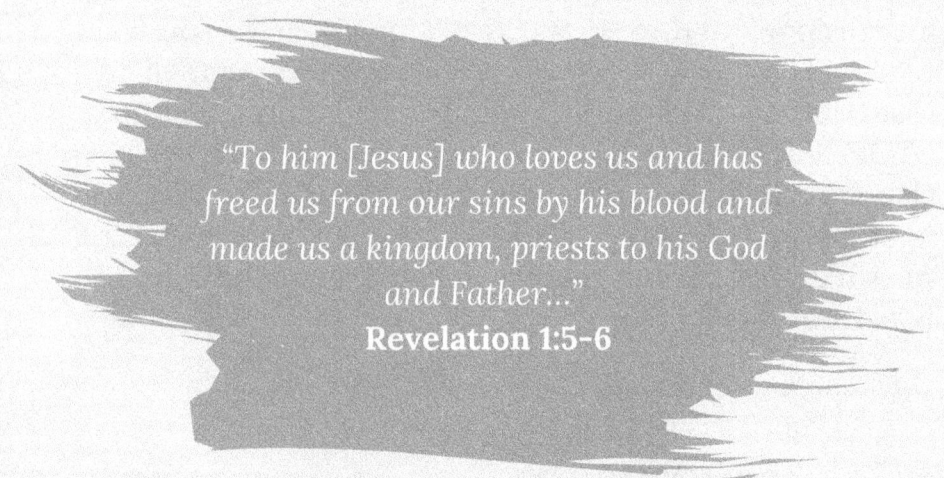

"To him [Jesus] who loves us and has freed us from our sins by his blood and made us a kingdom, priests to his God and Father..."
Revelation 1:5-6

Thank God for Jesus. This is why we must be intentional about spending our time on things above, referring to spiritual things, the things of God and not our natural selves and yearnings. Rebuke hunger for the world and sin, and set your minds on things above. Where you spend your time matters because that time will shape your heart and mind. If you want to see transformation, spend as much time seeking the Lord as you do the things that satisfy your flesh. This is the time to be a TRANSFORMER, not a CONFORMER.

#ChooseYeThisDay#GodMakesTheDifference#WhereAreYouSpendingYourTime #LessOfMeMoreOfYou

Song of the Day:
Ultimate Relationship-Donald Lawrence & Company Featuring Lalah Hathaway

Day 7

Wowwwwwwww!!! You made it one week on Consecration! Today is a day of celebration and reflection. Please take a moment to share what you have noticed or experienced over the last seven days or what you are expecting from God in the next seven days. Can't wait to read your testimony or your expectation! I'll start.... these past seven days, I've realized how distracted I can be with the things of the world: I've literally been intentional in hearing God. Sometimes social media can be overwhelming! I've been able to hear God and see His Hand more clearly. I expect that God is going to provide more direction in the next seven days for where and what He will have me to do...I'm excited to see what report is yielded when Day 14 comes forward. I am actually loving the intentionality of my relationship with God these days...I'm letting God truly have His way!

#AnIntentionalGod#HisPlanForMyLife
#GodsWillIsWhatIWant

**Song of the Day:
God's Will Is What I Want
Ricky Dillard**

Day 8

I come in writing already FULL 😩😭🥹!! Let me start by just declaring, God Is Real. In my study and prayer time this morning, God spoke to me that it's a Heart Condition. True change and true evolution come through the heart. Often times, we judge people and things based solely on appearance but God evaluates the heart. You've made the commitment and said to God that you want to be washed over again and made new. Well, He's going to start with your inner self and that change will bring forth the outer.

Here's where God made it so clear. I was reading 1 Samuel 16:7

"But the Lord said to Samuel, "Do not look at his appearance or at the height of his stature, because I have rejected him. For the Lord sees not as man sees; for man looks at the outward appearance, but the Lord looks at the heart.""

I wanted to know more so God said go back and read the entire chapter. 1 Samuel 16 is about Samuel searching for the next King of Israel. Samuel went to the house of Jesse who had eight sons. Watch that number eight right there, I'll be back to that reference. Jesse submitted 7 of his sons to be King, but God told Samuel that all of them were rejected. It's not that these sons didn't have physical or mental competency to do the job, but God was looking at the heart condition when He was making His decision. So, he rejected all seven that were put forth. Samuel asked Jesse to be sure, "Are all your sons here?" Jesse made it clear that his youngest, his eighth (ha, there it goes again) son was tending to the sheep. Samuel sent for David and while David was handsome and had beautiful eyes, He didn't look as we would think a king would look when standing alongside his brothers; however, when God is in you and has touched you and you have given Him your yes, genuinely, He will send confirmation of the plans that He has for you and place you in position to be used for His glory. Whewwwwww 😇 😰! God can use the least of these. God is looking inward at things that sometimes the human eye just can't see.

Now why am I messed up? Today is day 8 of consecration. 8 spiritually represents New Beginnings. I really thought my key verse would be Romans 12:2

> *"And be not conformed to this world: but be ye transformed by the renewing of your mind, that ye may prove what is that good, and acceptable, and perfect, will of God."*

But God had me dig deeper and read the entire book of 1 Samuel to find that on this 8th Day of Consecration, the 8th son of Jesse, David was chosen to be the next King. Now, David didn't immediately go into position. He was anointed and sent into service. That's another story for another day, but filled with so much meat for the soul!"

It's Day 8 and your new start is here. Open yourself to Him and ask God for the status of your heart. This can't be ordinary; you need EXTRAORDINARY and that love and change can only come from God. Does your heart reflect His will? His love? His posture? God's love can fill, touch, and change your heart so you can truly have a heart like thine.

#TheHeartOfTheMatter#AHeartCondition#Heart8ight
#HeartWashed

**Song of the Day:
Ordinary Just Won't Do-Commissioned**

Day 9

Have you ever been in a place where you really wanted to just draw closer to God? I really wanted to understand this God who soothes all my doubts, calms all my fears and loves me so much. Well, I've come to learn on this journey that the only way to truly know Him and be changed into the image of Him is to be in relationship with Him. It's really like dating that person who captures your eye. You spend time on the phone and aimlessly talk about any and everything. You're always wondering what that person is doing or if they would like something. You want to know their nature and really be connected with them. This is how we must pursue our relationship with God. Being married for currently over 11 years, I've found in some ways, I take on the nature of my wife. For instance, my wife loves chewing ice. It was never my thing. The more I hung around her, I found myself chewing ice. I'm so obsessed, I bought a nugget ice maker (aht aht, stop judging me lol). But isn't it crazy how being around someone, you take on their NATURE?

Imagine if we spend so much time with God, He totally changes our NATURE? Imagine if we spend our time with God, the creator, the one who knows the inner most parts of us, how that will bring about a change? . You MUST spend time talking to Him and allowing Him to talk to you. That second part can be challenging because we tend to ask God, but don't have the patience to allow Him to speak to us of His will. Prayer is simply an intimate conversation with the one who loves us unconditionally. He wants to talk to you and you talk with Him and the more time you spend with Him, God will change your nature. Psalm 90:12 says,

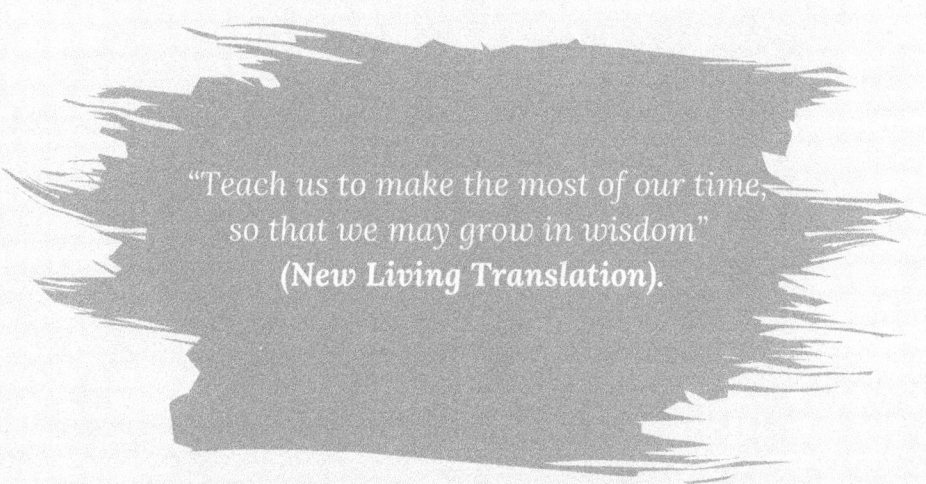

"Teach us to make the most of our time, so that we may grow in wisdom"
(New Living Translation).

Evaluate today, where are you spending your time in relationship to God? Are you making the right deposits in His account? You can't withdraw or receive a dividend on your investment, if you're not talking to or listening to God. I'm here to encourage you to sign up with the Bank of Jesus. It's profitable in every way you can imagine. You will have exponential growth because you're being guided by the CEO himself, our loving Lord and Savior, Jesus Christ.

And truly, the more that you spend time with Him, the more He can change your NATURE. Choose Ye this day. The choice is yours.

#ChangeMeOhGod#MoreLikeHim#ChangeYourNature #OnlyGodCanDoIt

**Song of the day:
Change Your Nature–BeBe and CeCe Winans**

Day 10

Yesterday, I was privileged with great offline conversation about the teaching from yesterday. The recurring theme, TIME MATTERS. I was sharing with the tribe the irony of living in a sinful world and wanting to be an example of Christ but having to invest and spend so much time in the world. From working to school to eating and other activities, we are immersed in this world. So how do we keep our hearts and our minds stayed on Jesus. As one tribe member asked, "make it make sense?" Lol absolutely. Let me try and help.

So why is this need or desire to sin such a battle if I love Jesus? It goes back to Adam and Eve in the Garden of Eden. The serpent led them to believe God wasn't being honest with them and by eating the forbidden fruit, there was better or more. Sounds so familiar right? Like the world now presents a fast flashy life and glitz and glam as the popular way for easy living. So, when Adam and Eve sinned, it corrupted the perfect NATURE that God created in us. This strategy of showing us flashy and telling us more is an old trick of the enemy. But thank God for Jesus. 🛐🙏.

He wants to change us from the INSIDE-OUT! If He can change our hearts and our inner man, it will naturally shape our choices, decisions and desires. That is why it's critical that we devote more of our time to Him. 2 Peter 1:3 NLT states, By His divine power, God has given us everything we need for living a godly life. We have received all of this by coming to know Him..

As the seasoned saints proclaimed, we must know God in the pardon of our sins. We must understand His love for us, His will for our lives, His ability and desire to make us new creatures in Him. Don't lose hope family, God has a plan for us, if we say yes and allow Him to do what only God can do.

I want to give you a personal assignment today. Take a piece of paper and for the last 48 hours, assess where have you been spending your time? Are you spending more time running after silver and gold and worldly passions, or do we intentionally ensure that we deposit doses of Jesus throughout our day? Having a relationship with Jesus and the gift of the Holy Spirit abiding in us is the only way that we can fight this temptation and desire to sin.

Ephesians 6:12 KJV always reminds us,

> *"For we wrestle not against flesh and blood, but against principalities, against powers, against the rulers of the darkness of this world, against spiritual wickedness in high places."*

Focus not on your behavior, focus on your NATURE. Get the heart and mind of God and I can ensure you my beloved, the behavior will naturally begin to shift. Yes, it's a process, but God's plan and process is always PERFECT. Choose His Will no matter how challenging it can get. And remember, His Will is always what's best.

#YourWillGod#TeamJesus#AWonderfulChange#ChangeYourNature

**Song of the Day:
Your Will-Darius Brooks**

Day 11

We have been on this journey of consecration and this morning, I'm being led to encourage YOU, Don't Give Up. Hang on in there because God has victory on the other side of this. There are periods in transformation where we know change is happening, but it may not seem as prevalent on the outside. But God is cleansing and rejuvenating YOU from the inside out so we have to keep meditating on His word day and night and not allowing our flesh to distract us from the finish line.

Transformation starts in the heart and the mind. Let's deal with the mind today. May I reMIND you what God thinks about you. Psalm 139:14 reMINDS us that we are fearfully and wonderfully made. We are made in the image of God and He makes all things well. When we receive Jesus, God doesn't just forgive our sins, He changes your NATURE. So, you have urges that lead you to sin. In your human flesh, you have a sinful nature; but thank God for your confession that He is Lord and you believe. Because of this, you become a NEW creature.

The enemy will attempt to tamper with your thoughts and make you believe God doesn't love you because of your struggles or is angry because you sinned. NO, God loves you in spite of all things. That's why He gives grace and mercy. He knew before you were formed the struggles you would encounter and that's why He said in Matthew 11:28, "Come unto me, all ye that labour and are heavy laden, and I will give you rest." Rest in His ability to change your heart and mind and to give you the strength to be just whom He predestined.

Whewwwww...this is good to me...Rest in Him family. What did I say yesterday, stop focusing on changing the behavior and let Him change your heart and mind. When the inner man is changed, the outer display will reflect the images of Christ which are love, peace, joy, happiness, gratefulness, gratitude, and one that reflects His Heart. 2 Corinthians 5:17 says,

"Therefore if any man be in Christ, he is a new creature: old things are passed away; behold, all things are become new."

You are blood washed, you are new, God has changed your NATURE. All because you said YES.

And this morning, maybe you fell off the wagon, well, recommit. Yes, right now. Just declare to the Father,

> "I need you God. Change my heart and my mind. Remove anything that's not like You. When I speak, allow me to speak well of YOU and myself because I am made in Your Image and therefore, I am fearfully and wonderfully made."

Today is the day that you are only allowed to speak what God has said about YOU. Eliminate the distractions, realign your MIND, and keep allowing God to change your NATURE from the inside out. Take one minute today and write down who God says you are. After you write them, speak them and declare them EVERYDAY. Allow your MIND to come in alignment with whom God has purposed you to be. Take back the power and authority God has given YOU. Goodbye Self-Saboteur and Hello New Creature!

#MindRegulation#SetYourMind#OnThingsAbove#HeartAndSoul

**Song of the Day:
All That God Said-Dr. Ed Montgomery**

Day 12

One of the best things about this period of consecration has been how my life has been coming into ALIGNMENT with God. I have been intentional about seeking God, hearing His voice, and honoring His word. It hasn't been easy. I literally have to remind myself of the commitments that I made to ensuring the best possible ride during this consecration. When I think of ALIGNMENT, I think about a car. The definition of ALIGNMENT is a group of objects, circumstances or people physically arranged in a straight line. Have you ever driven a car that's not in ALIGNMENT? While you are able to continue the journey, it's not the most efficient or comfortable ride. That car starts veering to the right or left 😄 and those tires are just as slick as a baby's bottom😄😄. It might still be going, but it's more risky and dangerous than ever before.

That's what it's like when our life is out of ALIGNMENT with the will of God. He's given us the machine (our body) but we must ensure that we spend time with the mechanic (God) so He can provide us the necessary tools and navigation for this journey called life.

Psalm 37:4 says,

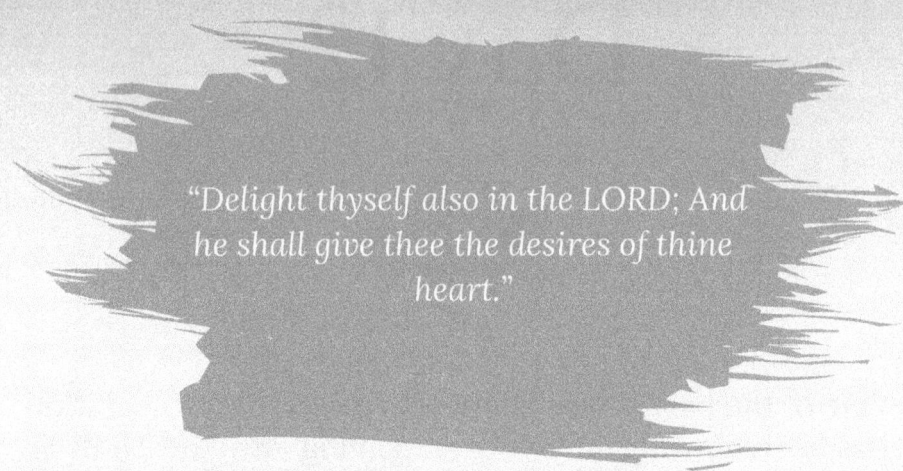

"Delight thyself also in the LORD; And he shall give thee the desires of thine heart."

The time you spend with God is so critical because how can He fix what's broken if you don't confess it? How can He tell you the plans that He has for you if you never open your heart to Him and allow Him to tell you about you. Sometimes we run from the mechanic because we know the car hasn't been serviced, it's too much service fees that will apply and we don't want the stress. Oh, but thank God for Jesus. He already paid for every sin, every transgression, every mess up because He loves YOU so much. But you wouldn't truly understand the depths of His love if you don't spend time with Him. And when you delight yourself in the Lord, He's going to upgrade YOU. He is the God of abundance so when you leave spending time with Him, you are renewed like the eagle and you can fly high with strength and tenacity.

Romans 12:1 says,

"I beseech you therefore, brethren, by the mercies of God, that ye present your bodies a living sacrifice, holy, acceptable unto God, which is your reasonable service."

" Commit to daily spending time in the presence of God and allowing Him to shape your heart and mind. Allow Him to upgrade your current life, to put you into ALIGNMENT with His will for your life. Don't allow the distractions of this world to take you out of ALIGNMENT on this journey. Stay in His presence and in His Will and watch God work for you.

#MakeYourAppointment#AlignmentAwaits #TimeMatters #AreYouOverdue

**Song of the Day:
I Delight In Your Presence
Born Again Church Mass Choir or Crossroads Tabernacle**

Day 13

Oh my beloved, I am writing while once again just being in awe of God. Yesterday was a travel day for me so I was either in a car or on flights literally for most of the day. Several things happened yesterday and I literally looked at it through the eyes of God. I found favor with the Delta ticket agent at the airport and I never waved a banner saying I'm a Kingdom Kid or asked for his favor. God just literally allowed His light to shine down. Last night, I was driving back from Charleston after my flight and God spoke directly to me about this consecration. At this point, the metamorphosis is occurring. You're no longer the caterpillar but if you have truly been following and seeking Him, internally you have probably been saying "something is different." Ah yes, my beloved, God is doing a new thing. This is the transformation and you're becoming that butterfly. You're a new creature and the old things have passed away. God has changed your NATURE🙌🙏. Thank you, JESUS!! It required you to be separated, consecrated, and dedicated.

This consecration removed me from what I was accustomed to and forced me to let God shine the light on my impurities. I saw strengths and areas where I needed to tighten up. I consecrated myself literally to the will and the way of God. I've been able to hear God in a way I've never heard. My ears are on HIS frequency. I dedicated myself to showing up every day, no matter what and becoming disciplined in the strengthening and conditioning exercises that He wanted me to do. Endurance makes a good soldier. We aren't even at day 21, but if you're like me, I see Him and I feel Him and I'm thankful. So now what, Jeffrey? Where do we go from here?

In my study time this morning, God instructed me to read Ephesians 5. 🙇😌🙆. So much good meat (Godly wisdom) is in there, but there were some verses that really struck gold for me. Ephesians 5:8 AMP says,

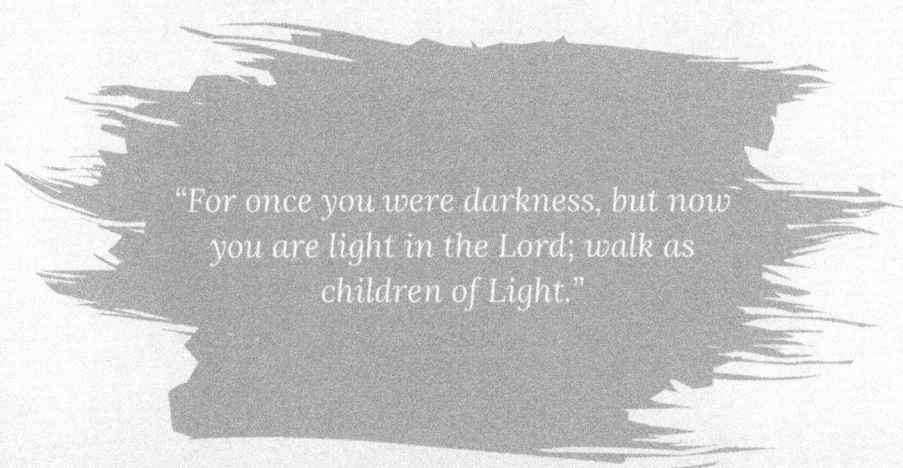

"For once you were darkness, but now you are light in the Lord; walk as children of Light."

You are not the same who you were 13 days ago because God is purifying your heart and your mind. You're aware of your choices and decisions.

You're intentional about how you move and where you spend your time. You're not the caterpillar who's slugging along and can only see limited options. You have been transformed by the renewing of your mind into a butterfly. You are seeing and thinking above because your view has changed. God did it 🙆‍♀️😊 OMG! If you're reading this in my voice you know I'm about to lose it. God gave a mandate through the words of Apostle Paul this morning. No, you shouldn't look like the world or move like them. That's darkness but you are light. Your presence changes the room. The love of Christ overflows that people desire to be in your presence.

And don't be afraid of this newness. Don't be afraid that the light has become so bright that you see this thing clearly, you see differently. And no, you're not better than anyone and you don't think of yourself higher than anyone else. Your motive is simply to please God and that light of love is shining through you. Ephesians 5:13 says,

> "But all things become visible when they are exposed by the light [of God's precepts], for it is light that makes everything visible."

God's light is beaming and you just have to be willing to let that light shine bright.

Not for people to praise you but for them to glorify God. Jesus instructed us to

> *"Let your light so shine before men, that they may see your good works, and glorify your Father which is in heaven."*
> **Matthew 5:16 KJV**

This change is simply to make you better and to make you an ambassador for Christ, not only in word but also in deed. In the coming days, we will discuss what that looks like, but I'm going to yield for now. Let's just chew on this today. I encourage you to read ALL of Ephesians 5. It will surely bless you. But congratulations so far, on this journey. Your metamorphosis has hit and it's time to spread your wings and prepare to fly as you have become a butterfly.

Fly, fly with the LIGHT!!

#NewMe #NewCreature #SomethingHappened

Song of the day:
Dedicated-Bishop Nathaniel Bond and The DHP Mass Choir

Day 14

Wowwwwwwww! We have made it two whole weeks! 14 days of total commitment to the King of Kings. I can truly say it's been totally life changing. There have been moments where you may have wanted to give up or throw in the towel, but look at you. You're still standing!! Which simply means there is more race for you to run. My desire is that God blows your mind in these last 7 days. I'm praying for powerful testimonies, supernatural blessings, a renewal of your love and passion for Christ and an updated prescription on your eyesight for God. What is your level of expectation going into these last 7 days?

In my study today, I was reading in Matthew 9 about the blind men who followed Jesus and begged for mercy. They were blind and could not see. "Then touched their eyes, saying,

> "According to your faith, be it unto you."
> **Matthew 9:29 KJV**

Where is your faith family? He told the men according to their faith, it shall be. Well, I just truly believe God can do the impossible in these last 7 days. And there is no room to doubt Him. Any doubt must be thrown into the sea of forgetfulness.

So, take this day and write down what you're believing God for these last seven days. More trust in His word, more consistency in your study time, or whatever it is. By your faith so shall it be, in the name of Jesus. Write it down, meditate on it, decree and declare it and let's finish strong in these next seven days. I'm so excited about the testimonies to come. It's all happening on the other side of this.

#TheOtherSide#NeverTheSame#TheLastLeg #ByYourFaith

Song of the Day:
The Other Side Of This- Pastor Angie Cleveland

Day 15

The journey of this spiritual metamorphosis that is taking place is not one that will last 21 days and we will be done. Oh no, this is simply the setup for continual living. We must in all things daily exercise out this walk with Christ. So think about it this way, what started as an egg, developed into a larva(caterpillar), then transformed into a pupa, and now you're a beautiful butterfly. What a change God has made all because YOU chose to allow Him to change you from the INSIDE-OUT. But this change is not about YOU. It's about God getting the glory in all things. He needs you to be a light, to be an example that will draw men unto Him. Romans 12:1 AMP states, "Therefore I urge you, brothers and sisters, by the mercies of God, to present your bodies [dedicating all of yourselves, set apart] as a living sacrifice, holy and well-pleasing to God, which is your rational (logical, intelligent) act of worship."

So how does one stay true to this commitment to Christ while living in a sinful world? I'm so glad you asked lol... Let's Explore.

Because God has changed your inner man and His Holy Spirit now abides inside of you, your actions will become different. While in our natural flesh, we are of a sinful nature, Apostle Paul teaches us in Galatians 5 that we have freedom in Christ who died and rose so that we can be free. This does not give us a license to sin and live any kind of way. We must walk in the spirit and allow the spirit to be our guide. In fact, Galatians 5:17 says,

> "the flesh desires what is contrary to the Spirit, and the Spirit what is contrary to the flesh."

So you can be led by the flesh, or you can be led by the Spirit of God, but you can't be led by both. Choose ye this day. I'm choosing to be led by the spirit. Stop right now and openly declare, who you are choosing to lead you, the flesh or the Holy Spirit?

The Fruit of the Spirit is listed in Galatians 5—love, joy, peace, patience, kindness, goodness, faithfulness, gentleness, and self-control.

Over these last 6 days of consecration, we are going to explore the fruit of the spirit and ensure that we fully understand the evidence that should be the residue that we deposit into the earth.

We will not focus on chasing after the fruit, but on how our relationship with God will allow the fruit to be on full display. Remember, we NEVER chase after things, we chase after GOD because He is the creator of all things. The fruit of the spirit is simply the evidence of being connected to God. And as we study and explore, if you feel that the fruit isn't on full display, this will ensure that you're always checking your connection and that your connection to Christ is always in place.

#CheckYourConnection#OneFruitManyParts #ChangeIsNecessary #MakeADecision

Song of the day:
Come Fill This Place-Beverly Crawford

Day 16

Welcome back family. You know, the fact that you have been showing up daily and being ALL IN.... Wow, I celebrate YOU. And the evidence is beginning to show. Oh, I know you've seen it. You're more aware of your responses, you have a keen sense of where your time is being spent, and you have this eagerness to just please God and be an example of Him. I'm not surprised at all. What you feed is what will grow and these past 16 days, you have fed your spirit man word and attention and development. That muscle is STRONG. Yasssssssss!! I'm dancing in the spirit about what God is doing. Your fruit is showing because you're spending time with God and His presence dwells within YOU. Don't be fooled, this doesn't mean you won't sin or have a desire to sin because you are of sinful nature. YOU will sin please understand that. However, the goal is that your lifestyle is a reflection of God and the goodness and grace of God. So, Jeffrey, you talk about this evidence, what is it? Well Apostle Paul teaches us that it's the fruit of the spirit. n simple terms, it's the evidence that we are spending time with God and He is moving and working in our hearts and minds.I Let's examine some of the evidence that will appear.

Today, let's focus on LOVE and Joy.

LOVE is the most important attribute to have as a believer in the body of Christ. God is LOVE. He's the ultimate and we need LOVE in all things. Apostle Paul states in 1 Corinthians 13 we can do good works, speak in tongues, all these various things but if we don't have LOVE, we are like a clashing cymbal. Now see, my ears are bothered already because imagine a clashing cymbal - just endless noise with no direct and focused sound. As we walk and grow with Christ, our lives gain purpose and the LOVE of God permeates on the inside and shines on the outside. LOVE begins to show through our words and actions because God is Love and He abides in us. 1 Corinthians 13:4-8 says,

> "Love is patient, love is kind. It does not envy, it does not boast, it is not proud. It does not dishonor others, it is not self-seeking, it is not easily angered, and it keeps no record of wrongs. LOVE does not delight in evil, but rejoices with the truth. It always protects, always trusts, always hopes, always perseveres. Love never fails..."

However you twist it or turn it, LOVE WINS. How much we LOVE determines how well we know God, therefore, the more we know God the more LOVE will flow through our life.

#LetLoveRule

Joy is the second attribute of the fruit of the spirit. Don't get JOY and happiness confused. Happiness is a temporary emotion, but JOY is eternal. As believers, we place our hope on things eternal and even though times may be challenging or rough, we still have JOY because we know God is always with us. Philippians 4:4 says,

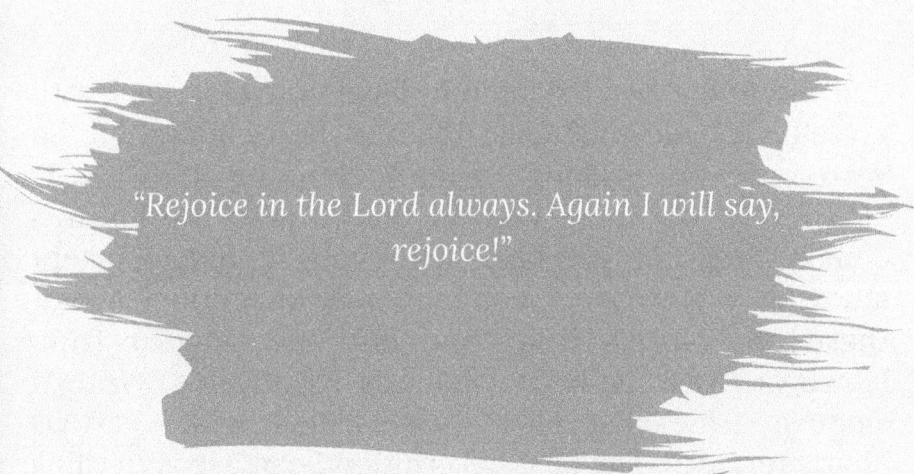

"Rejoice in the Lord always. Again I will say, rejoice!"

No matter what the enemy may try to throw in your path, we have JOY in knowing that God shall always get the victory in every circumstance. We don't rejoice in the fact that trouble has arisen, we rejoice because we know the one who knows all and controls all. It reminds me of the old spiritual, "This joy I have, the world didn't give it and the world can't take it away." Hold on to your JOY!

#JoyLikeNoneOther

**Song of the Day:
Spiritual-Donald Lawrence & Company**

Day 17

Call me crazy but I definitely have conversations with myself. Oh, you too? Glad I'm not the only one lol. So yesterday I'm walking around shouting EVIDENCE, EVIDENCE. My mind was on the Fruit of the Spirit. I couldn't wait to get back with you all today. I kept studying yesterday. A common misconception is that these are various fruits and not one singular fruit. However, when Apostle Paul was writing, he wrote it singular, meaning it's one fruit, with various characteristics. The best description I can use is to think of an orange. I can peel slices out of the orange. If I take a slice out, I can still identify that it's an orange. These behaviors we're studying are just EVIDENCE that you're walking in the spirit. So, let's turn our attention back to Galatians 5 and we are going to focus on PEACE and PATIENCE.

In a world that is full of calamity and confusion, it's truly a blessed assurance to know that we have PEACE. PEACE is not saying I go in my house and close my door and there is silence. That's not the PEACE Apostle Paul was referencing. It's a confidence in the God that we serve and His ability to answer every prayer and petition before Him.

As the METAMORPHOSIS has taken place, your eyesight and vision has changed. You no longer look at situations in the natural world, but you observe with your spiritual eye and you understand that God has the final say. Philippians 4:7 AMP says,

> "And the peace of God [that peace which reassures the heart, that peace] which transcends all understanding, [that peace which] stands guard over your hearts and your minds in Christ Jesus [is yours]."

No matter what trial I may be facing, no matter what situation may arise, I have a PEACE that can only come from God that He will never fail. Your doctor gives you a negative report. I have PEACE. Your job lays you off, I have PEACE. You lost someone who was near and dear to your heart. I have PEACE. Whewwwwww, thank you JESUSSSSSSSS 🙌🙏. I have an assurance, that come hell or high water, I will not drown and I will not crumble because I have the PEACE that only God can give. God, I thank you. (Sorry y'all, I had a moment.) But think about it family, we get this peace only because we abide in Him.

John 16:33 AMP says,

"I have told you these things, so that in Me you may have [perfect] peace. In the world you have tribulation and distress and suffering, but be courageous [be confident, be undaunted, be filled with joy]; I have overcome the world." [My conquest is accomplished, My victory abiding.]"

This peace only comes for those who are in God. Those who walk in the spirit and abide with Him. It's a lifestyle. There's an old proverb that says" Birds of a feather flock together." Well, I'm flocking with my Savior, ha ha! I'm flocking and walking with the Prince of Peace. Through Him, I gain the PEACE that surpasses all understanding. Stretch your hand to God and when you place your hand in His, watch the PEACE and comfort that shall manifest upon you.

Another characteristic of this fruit is PATIENCE. Oh boy oh boy. YOU don't like to be PATIENT lol. It's okay, we don't judge over here (currently giving you the side eye lol). Nah, but we all have that struggle. We are conditioned in a world where everything is instant and sudden and right now.

However, when we are walking in the spirit, we should have PATIENCE in the same way that God is PATIENT with us. We mess up time and time again, but God is so loving and so PATIENT with us. We should extend that same grace in our walk with Christ because the goal is to be like HIM. And when we are abiding in Him, the EVIDENCE of that time will appear not just with people, but PATIENT with the walk and journey that we are on. Some biblical translations say "long suffering" as opposed to "patient." So what happens when we do the right thing and we are living right and trying to walk this thing out the way God commanded and we are still hit with afflictions? Do we give up and throw in the towel, NOOOOOOOO! We must remember the sacrifice that God made and the promises written in His word, and have PATIENCE that a perfect end is to come.
1 Peter 2:20 NIV states,

, "But how is it to your credit if you receive a beating for doing wrong and endure it? But if you suffer for doing good and you endure it, this is commendable before God."

When you endure, even when it seems like those around you are doing wrong and prospering, please my beloved, know that God sees and great is your reward.

Trust the process, be confident in the God WE serve and let that EVIDENCE of your fruit shine even more as you endure towards the perfect end.

#KeepOnWalking

Song of the Day:
Father I Stretch-Kim Burrell
Walking-Mary Mary

Day 18

Three days from the conclusion of the matter…Wow, what a journey. I'm in two places right now. Ready to hear the testimonies that will come out of this consecration and not wanting it to end because there is so much meat to explore in the word of God. It's truly been refreshing and life changing. We continue our exploration into the fruit of the spirit and today we focus on GENTLENESS and GOODNESS.

The world we live in fosters a theory that in order to be heard and stand out, you must be loud and harsh in tone. We take pride in someone saying, "oh he sets the house in order" or "oh, she doesn't play" all because we are nasty and downright mean. There is a way that seems right unto man, but is it the way of the Kingdom. GENTLENESS is the way of the Father because even in our wrong, His LOVE for us draws us back to the way that is right. Philippians 4:5 says, "Let your gentleness be evident to all. The Lord is near." Our spirit man should be so aligned with God that even in tense moments, the GENTLENESS of God shines through.

We are flesh so of course we are going to become frustrated and annoyed at times, but we must always allow our spirit man to rise up. Even when we need to provide corrections, there is a way to do it and it doesn't take us being harsh and brash. Proverbs 15:4 says, "The soothing tongue is a tree of life, but a perverse tongue crushes the spirit." Our words should uplift and encourage. They should motivate and inspire just as Christ motivates us to continue in the race even when we at times want to throw in the towel. Ask yourself, am I harming you or watering you with my words, with my tone, with the spirit in which I speak?

Another fruit of the spirit is GOODNESS. If I am transparent, this one truly excites me. I'm always trying to find ways to be good to someone. It literally thrills my soul. That's the way of our Father. God's GOODNESS is everlasting and we can't even put a cap on the abundance of GOODNESS He grants to us. David says in Psalm 23:6 KJV,

"Surely goodness and mercy shall follow me all the days of my life: And I will dwell in the house of the LORD forever."

The GOODNESS of man has limits but the GOODNESS of God never runs out. The world will lead us to believe that we reciprocate the behavior that one gives us. Oh, y'all know the famous line," I'm matching energy." It sounds cute, but that's just as wrong as two left shoes. Kingdom citizens don't match energy. Jesus says in Matthew 7:12 NIV,

"So in everything, do to others what you would have them do to you, for this sums up the Law and the Prophets."

That means we set the trend, we set the temperature, we are the guide for others to follow. And if we are walking in the spirit and God is shining, they will see the will and way of God. God does good no matter what and we are to always be like Him.

#WaterWithWords #GoodnessOfGod

**Song of the Day:
Words-Blanche McAllister-Dykes
& Goodness of God-CeCe Winans**

Day 19

Well thank you God for another day! YOU are still in the land of the living and that means another opportunity to share with the world the Goodness of God. It's another opportunity to reflect the heart of Jesus not just in words, but also in deeds. As we dive into our study for today, truly ask yourself, "Am I truly a reflection of the love of Jesus?" Let's dive right in.

Our relationship with the Holy Spirit allows for evidence of that relationship to be on full display. Here is the thing family, it's easy to wave the banner of Jesus when all is well, but what happens when someone makes you upset, your boss yells at you, someone cuts you off in traffic, your spouse forgets to pick up their clothes from off the chair (sorry Lady H😂), but at these moments, are we still able to walk in the fruit of the spirit and show KINDNESS. Oh yes, good old plain and simple KINDNESS. Hmmmm, but is it really so simple my beloved? 1 Corinthians 13:4a NIV says, "Love is patient, Love is Kind". It's easy to love and be KIND when things are right, what about when things are shaky? The true test is to show KINDNESS even when we want to lash out and give someone a piece of our mind.

That's not the way of Christ. He set the entire blueprint. Remember when Jesus was betrayed by one of his closest followers and then people made false statements about Him just so they could arrest and kill Him? Talk about your back being against the wall! ! But what did Jesus do? He Said NOTHING. He stood strong in His faith and trusted the will of God for His life. Yooooooo, I'm not making this up. 1 Peter 2:22-23 NIV says, "He committed no sin, and no deceit was found in His mouth." When they hurled their insults at Him, He did not retaliate; when He suffered, He made no threats. Instead, He entrusted Himself to Him who judges justly." Even while suffering, Jesus extended KINDNESS because He understood the assignment, as the young people say. He realized that it's bigger than Him. A verse I live by and truly enables me to walk in true KINDNESS is "Be kind and helpful to one another, tender-hearted [compassionate, understanding], forgiving one another [readily and freely], just as God in Christ also forgave you." Ephesians 4:32 AMP. We serve a God who extends KINDNESS to all of us and it's our job to be a reflection of this. #WithLovingKindness

Which leads us to FAITHFULNESS. Being fully committed to God no matter the circumstances. Our FAITHFULNESS to His plan and His agenda even when it gets challenging is key to walking in the spirit. You can't abandon ship when things don't go your way. The word of God tells us that we must endure like a follower of Jesus. But Jeffrey, how do I juggle the struggles of everyday life and remain faithful and committed to God? It's not easy and this is why we MUST stay in the Word and trust the plans that God has for us.

FAITHFULNESS is built out of FAITH. Where is your FAITH my beloved?
Romans 10:17 KJV says,

"So then faith cometh by hearing, and hearing by the word of God."

Aweeeee, it's coming full circle. Daily we must be in our word and understand what God has done and what God will continue to do. We will see the miracles and how God has never failed. We can reflect on our lives and how He's shown up every single time just in the nick of time. This will build our FAITH and therein cause our FAITHFULNESS to God and His Kingdom to reign over our lives. So I ask you again, WHERE IS YOUR FAITH?

#FaithfulIsOurGod

**Song of the Day:
JeKalyn Carr-Power Of Love
Pastor Hezekiah Walker-Faithful Is Our God**

Day 20

Do you understand the power of your YES? Think about that for a moment? When you give God your YES and commit to a life that is in alignment with His will, the impact that your life can have for the Kingdom is powerful. That's why the exploration into the fruit of the spirit has been so refreshing. We can't just give God a YES, we must understand the guidelines for daily living so we can be a total reflection of Him. Philippians 2:5 KJV says, "Let this mind be in you, which was also in Christ Jesus:" Walking in the spirit ensures that our mind is always set on things above. It's a pursuit for righteousness. It's literally saying, "God, I truly want to please You and only You." So the fruit of the spirit is that gentle reminder because when our flesh rises up, our mind will jump to the fruit which makes us question if our actions are in alignment with God.

This leads us to our final fruit of the spirit, SELF-CONTROL. Listen beloved, this is one that I can say I appreciate growing into. The world will lead you to believe you should have what you want and live your way and do YOU.Hmmmmm, wisdom has changed my heart and mind on that.

I can't do Jeffrey. I have to do God. What is His will and desire for me? That's the posture we should have which is why SELF-CONTROL or TEMPERANCE is so important.

2 Timothy 1:7 NIV says,

> *"For the Spirit God gave us does not make us timid, but gives us power, love and self-discipline."*

We must as believers know how to say yes to the good and no to the bad. We must have TEMPERANCE over the words that come out our mouths, the things we watch on television, and even the places our feet may trod. Let's be clear my beloved, YOU can't go everywhere. Having a mind that's in Christ allows us to be SELF-DISCIPLINED. When I say God has a sense of humor even down to parenting. Our Heavenly Father gives YOU all the tools, but He's going to place the final decision in YOUR hands. This is why our connection with the Holy Spirit is KEY. The Holy Spirit is our Comforter, our Guide, our reminder to pursue the things of the spirit and not the things of the flesh. The Holy Spirit cleans us from the inside out and reaches those places that we can't and makes us clean. If SELF-CONTROL is a challenge, give it to God and watch Him turn things around.

Remember this, there is nothing too dirty that God can't make worthy...whewwwwww! When we walk in the spirit, God makes us clean, new, and whole again. Thank You, Jesus, for your never-ending love. Thank you for making us clean. Thank you for the Fruit of the Spirit. And if we walk in the spirit, we will not fulfill the lust of the flesh. Just say this before we go: Lord, let YOUR spirit, DWELL IN ME. It is so, in Jesus' name, AMEN!!

#CleanLiving #FruitIsGood #EatWell

Song of the Day:
Clean-Natalie Grant
& Refiner-Maverick City Music featuring Chandler Moore & Steffany Gretzinger

Day 21

Wowwwwwww!!! All I can do is praise God for what He has done. 21 Days of praying, fasting, trusting, intentional living, 21 Days of Recommitment back to God. Look what the Lord has done. I'm just in a posture of gratefulness. I'm just full thinking about how God has truly made a change in my life over these last 21 days. When you really sit down and reflect on this 21-day consecration, you will realize how far you have come. Can you believe how distracted we have become with the things of the world? Having that structure, having that discipline, having that commitment to say, "God, you're first." And even more, just wanting to please Him and live for Him totally. Hear me my fellow believers, don't lose your FIRE. Don't lose the spark that has now ignited inside of you. God has allowed you to have a clear vision to see the path and plans He has for you. It's time to shine and build the Kingdom like never before. You cannot afford to allow anything to distract you from how far you have come. Tests and trials will come, but 2 Timothy 2:3 KJV states," Thou therefore endure hardness, as a good soldier of Jesus Christ." These 21 days have helped you identify who you are in the Kingdom.

Praise God for the journey and get ready, because the best is yet to come. Get ready for The Conclusion of the Matter! To God be all the glory! #Amen #ItIsFinished

Song of the Day:
Amen-Pastor Mike Jr.
The Best Is Yet To Come-Donald Lawrence

The Conclusion of the Matter

If you've journeyed with us through these 21 days, let me first congratulate you on being a part of something truly transformative. A few days before the fast began, Jeffrey and I were on the phone, and I shared that I felt led to embark on a 21-day fast. To my surprise, Jeffrey started shouting—he told me that God had been leading him to do the very same thing! We partnered together in obedience, and look at what God has birthed through this experience.

As you journeyed through this book, I believe a supernatural transformation has already been set in motion in your life. Jeffrey takes us on an in-depth exploration of prayer, and one thing is certain. It is impossible to stay in the presence of God and remain the same. Prayer is a divine key—one that unlocks the very portals of heaven.

We were created to dwell in His presence! Prayer awakens the creative genius within you, and as you seek God through prayer and fasting, He releases strategies, revelation, and wisdom. This journey is one of faith, not sight!

Now, as you conclude this time of consecration, let me declare over you that doubt and unbelief must be removed! Watch as your faith continues to rise and strengthen. Distractions that once clouded your focus are destroyed and clarity will remain. Your heart is now set on things above and God will continue to reveal great and mighty things to you. Condemnation is broken —shame and guilt no longer have a hold on you! You are made in His image, in His likeness, and you will walk boldly in the authority He has given you. Everything God has spoken and instructed during this time of fasting and consecration will manifest as you walk it out in obedience! (Matthew 17:21 KJV)

Throughout this book, Jeffrey has emphasized transformation, and that is where true change happens. Every lie the enemy has spoken over you is canceled! Every insecurity that once held you back is gone! You have been empowered to take control of your thoughts and emotions. God has given you dominion, authority, and power to experience continual victory. Your spirit man is strong, equipped to overcome anything life may throw your way. Let this mind be in you, which was also in Christ Jesus! (Philippians 2:5 KJV)

Let this book serve as a reminder and encouragement to live a life of consecration—this is your secret weapon.

Jeffrey, thank you for taking us on this journey with you. Your obedience to God will impact countless lives. I pray that every person who reads this book experiences the supernatural power of God resting upon them. We love you, son!
~Bishop Anthony Gibson

In conclusion, may the words of this song be a blessing to you: "God is Good (Live)" by Jonathan McReynolds. May it serve as a reminder of His faithfulness, grace, and the transformation He has begun in your life.

About The Author

It's no secret to anyone that when Jeffrey Lampkin enters the room, his warm heart and bubbly personality will make even the darkest day a bright one. A native of Manning, SC, Jeffrey joined the WACH Fox Good Day Columbia Team in 2008 as an Idol Correspondent after a successful run on Season 7 of the hit TV Show, American Idol. Jeffrey continued to become a must-see for the viewers and transitioned to Entertainment Reporter for Good Day Columbia. With much fanfare, Jeffrey became the host of the The Jeffrey Lampkin Show, the #1 Television Show on Sunday Morning for 6 Seasons.

A sought after event host and speaker, Jeffrey graduated from Manning High School in 2000. He received a Bachelor's Degree in Sociology from Newberry College and a Master's Degree in Human Resource Management from Webster University.

Jeffrey wears many hats. In addition to his work with Good Day Columbia, he is currently the host of Sunday Morning Gospel with Jeffrey Lampkin, which is currently the Number 1 Sunday Morning Radio Show, and airs weekly from 6a-10a on 101.3 The Big DM and the Number 1 Saturday morning show, Mister Lampkin's Neighborhood, Saturday mornings, 8a-10. He serves as the Public Information Officer/Deputy Coroner for the Richland County Coroners Office. He is the owner and operator of Jeffrey Lampkin's Country Boy Kitchen and Country Boy Bistro, both in Sumter SC and Bishopville SC, Co Owner and Marketing Director for The Lampkin Law Firm, Praise and Worship Leader at Grace Cathedral Sumter SC, and an award winning Choir Director, presently directing the Award Winning, Francis Marion University Young Gifted and Blessed Gospel Choir.

Jeffrey is a proud member Of the illustrious Kappa Alpha Psi. Fraternity INC. Jeffrey has received numerous awards, appeared on international and national television, and shared stages with countless political figures, artists, actors and actresses and more. Most recently, he was featured on Good Morning America not once, but twice sharing his passion for God and his music.

Jeffrey is happily married to Attorney Harriet Huell Lampkin. They reside in Elgin, South Carolina and are the proud parents of a cute chihuahua named Diamond Elizabeth Lampkin.

Jeffrey's passion for the People and his desire to see someone smile, give him the drive to make every day and every moment count.

As Jeffrey would say…Because God is the Greatest Power, You Shall Not Be Defeated!

INSIDE OUT BY JEFFREY LAMPKIN

Have you ever struggled to break free from bad habits, only to find yourself falling short time and time again? The journey to transformation can feel overwhelming, and consistency seems just out of reach. You may even find yourself thinking, If only someone understood my struggle.

In this powerful 21-day spiritual journey, **American Idol Finalist Jeffrey Lampkin** invites you to walk alongside him as he peels back the layers of his own life, revealing raw and relatable moments of faith, perseverance, and breakthrough. Through daily reflections, Lampkin leads you toward a deeper understanding of God and the life-changing power of transformation.

Metamorphosis has finally come. This daily devotional will not only challenge and inspire you but also guide you to your personal exodus—your victory awaits.

REVIEWS

It is amazing how much we find, concerning our needs from Almighty God, that we haven't necessarily aligned ourselves to. It's good to know that it's never too late, especially when it comes to Him, making us better. The words on these pages give true testimony to the awesomeness of God and his love for us, while providing practical solutions in a complicated world. Read and don't forget to tell...it's what makes the difference EVERY time. Great stuff!😊

-Kim Burrell, Grammy-Nominated, Recording Artist

In a climate of conflict, confusion, and chaos; it is essential that we keep a consistent devotion with God! "Inside Out" is a must read! God has given Jeffrey Lampkin a tool for us to daily walk with Him "in the cool of the day!" As you commit to these 21 days, you will be transformed from the "Inside Out!" It's your time to emerge!

-Pastor Johnny Brown, The Genesis Church (North Carolina)

Struggling to balance life in a world full of distractions while keeping your heart and mind on Jesus? Jeffrey Lampkin's, Inside Out challenges you to examine where you invest your time and align with God's will. Through biblical wisdom, deep reflections, and practical exercises, this journey isn't just about changing behavior—it's about true transformation from the inside out. Your renewal starts now!

-Elder Frank Dyer, COO/Executive Pastor, Potter's House Dallas

www.ingramcontent.com/pod-product-compliance
Lightning Source LLC
Chambersburg PA
CBHW032213040426
42449CB00005B/580